Overlooked Flower

Seriana Gamble

I dedicate this to my mom for believing in me, past relationships that taught me to love myself harder, my siblings for being the light of my life, and family and friends that encouraged me to excel.

Table of Contents

Infatuation and Love

Path of Love

I want to be loved as much as Americans
love coke
Or as much as puppies love getting their
belly rubbed
Or as much as hoes love sex
Well, you get the point
I want that raw love that can't be tainted
The kind you dream about but never
crosses your path
That kind of love that people part their lips
in shock
After you tell them how long you been
intertwined
Yet you feel like you met them yesterday
kind of love
The kind of love where my heart flutters at
the mention of your name
But not the kind of flutter you get with a
crush
Nah, that warm sensation flowing through
your body kind of feeling
Yea that kind of love
You know that kind of love where you still
fight, but at the end
You think being without that person would
be worse than the fight itself
The kind of love you tell everyone you meet
The kind of love that lifts you off your feet
Not the generic snap, crackle, pop kind

But the one that gives you a new feeling
every time the minute hand goes by
The one that has you wishing time would
stop
So you could hold the moment with just
you two
The kind of love that makes you a better
you
That's the kind of love I want in my life
The kind of love that you never want to die
I don't want the ones that come and go out
like the candle in the night
Or the one that gets you feeling like an
abandoned old toy after Christmas
Not the one that keeps you up at night
Because you constantly continue to fight
Not the toxic "love" that consumes your
life
Not the love that nags you like a bug bite

I thought it was love, but that's just a lie
I want real love
The one where you just look at each other
and know you found the key
That's the love I want
That's where I want to be.

<u>Replay</u>

Your words flow through my phone
Your memories float through my head
Your voice rings in my ears
And here I am lying in bed
Thinking of you and wondering if you're
thinking of me
Is this something serious or is this a just a
fling?
I wake up to your text and go to sleep on
your goodnight wishes
When we are together, it's like my heart
stops and listens
To every laugh you release, every joke you
make
Every simple movement you do, brings a
smile to my face
When you are away, you cloud my thoughts
I wonder if I'm letting myself get too far
I don't verbally express how I feel because
then I would be vulnerable
But inside I'm shaking to yell the truth
I'm falling for you and I don't know what to
do
Is the feelings I have for you true or is
covering up an old wound
The kiss you lay upon my lips makes me
forget
Everything that matters in life instead
I let you hold me while I complain

But to be honest this affection has me going
insane
What if this is just a game?
What if I'm being played?
What if the story stays the same?
Should I just stay in my lane?
Or jump in the car with you and take that
ride?
I can't decide.
You kiss me again and I drift back to reality
Your love seems true to me
I guess we will just have to wait and see
But for now, time has stopped, and you are
facing me
Waiting patiently
For me to open my heart to you and to stop
worrying about the little things.
Old experiences continue to bring me pain
As I try not to let that interfere with my
future plans
You hold my hand
And my worries disappear all over again.

A Dangerous Game

You got my heart fluttering
Beating like the sound of a bass I drum
Flapping as fast as the wings of a
hummingbird
Speeding and flooding with blood with just
the simple site of you
Blood pressure rising through the roof, I
just want you

You got my mind racing
Running over the horizon and passing by
like a shooting star
Feel like I'm going crazy because oh baby I
want you to be mine
Feel like I'm tripping because the thought
of you has me doped up
My nerves sending signals because all I'm
feeling is your love
I'm distracted by your magic

You got my eyes gazing
Stuck on your beautiful brown eyes as they
gaze in my soul
Making me nervous as you look me over
Can't look at you for too long or I get lost
Looking over pictures of you endlessly so I
can remember you
Just in case your greatness comes to an end

But my eyes search for a way out

But I've already fallen in

You got my hands wandering
Trying to grasp onto the reality you keep
pulling me from
Holding onto your hair to pull you in
Feeling for your warmth and hoping you
won't hurt me again
Wandering over the text that makes my lips
spread from end to end

You got my toes curling
With the thoughts of you
Your hands traveling over the areas that are
off limits to anyone else's view
You make me feel brand new
I'm convinced that you deliver sensations
that I want to feel again and again

You make me smile
Like no other
Your voice, your hugs, your love
Makes me want to open up and give you the
world
Makes me feel like I'm a little girl
And you don't even know that I'm falling in
love

So why do I hesitate or feel like this is
another phase?

Because I find it hard to trust.

Hard to love
Hard to let another dude just treat me like a
drug
Take as needed and when you're trying to
escape
But once you get your high, you leave me to
burn out and decay
I am afraid that your words are not true and
you aren't really you
That the fall will hurt when I finally land
And you're just here to get your dick in
So I hesitate when you say something nice
Or when you say you want to be mine
Because I'm either going to have to take a
leap of faith
Or land on my face
Is this love safe?

In Deep

Mixed Emotions

Coming, Going,
I'm falling for you.
I talk to other people, but I still can't
surpass this truth
I'm falling for you.
You annoy me, but the sound of your voice
melts the ice around my heart.
The compassion you show
when times are tough
makes my life feel less rough.
Your jokes were enough-
I'm falling for you
, but then again… I'm not.
You flip like a coin or a feather in a breeze.
One day you're attentive and jolly
paying me the attention I need
then you act like my father and leave-
I stop falling for you.
I start to harden and turn
Like bread left out in the sun.
I'm tired, overworked, and used.
All I wanted was you
Not for my emotions to be abused.
I was falling for you, but now
I'm just confused.
You say one thing, but do another
I just wish you were as loyal as my mother
But like a penny, the value of your words is
close to none.

But the coin still seems to be in circulation.
.you for falling I'm

I bend backwards trying to meet you
halfway.
Your love spreads like a wildfire on dry
terrain
And somehow I always get burnt by the
flames.
I am becoming drained.... Did I make a
mistake?
It might be too late.
I've fallen for you.

<u>2 truths 1 lie</u>

Let's play an old-time game
And see if my answers remain the same
I walked down legacy waiting for the
answers to come to me
I tuned out the world, just my thoughts and
my soul
And I thought why not announce 2 truths
and 1 lie…
Well as it begins, I shall say I wish I never
said "let's just be friends"
I think about you constantly and get hella
jealous when you claim to be hanging with
"friends"
Because you see that's how you and I began.
So my mind wanders around
the idea of you hanging under this umbrella
of an ambiguous title.
For in my mind I already labeled you as my
secret to keep.
The apple that was forbidden to eat or
the grade that you don't want your parents
to see.
But as my secret leaves my grasp I rather
have you back.
Well may be too late so time to continue
this game-
I have become vulnerable and open because
of you.

Something I hate to admit, but it's true. It
makes me scared,
Unsure, and weary. I have always made it a
mission to keep my soul safe
And to maintain a healthy and focused
brain, but the ink from your leaking heart
tainted it.
I been fainted, but yet I pushed you away.
It's all the same.
I loved the way you weren't afraid to tell me
how you felt
even if it meant you getting an
unreciprocated response. You still took the
leap
And awaited my response. I am sorry I did
you wrong.
I don't know how these things work so I
don't try, but rather keep my distance
Until it passes by. When honestly, I didn't
want to say goodbye.
I thought it was an infatuation of the time
and just silly butterflies.
I thought I wanted a guy who wore ties or
dressed up sometimes, but
I realize all I care about it is that you
support me in my life..
That you stop a piece of your day just to
make sure I'm alright. That you say I'm
beautiful even
when I look like a moldy piece of meat.
Unpleasant and something no one would
dare eat.

Yea you do things that get on my nerves or
bother me unintentionally, but it made me
realize you are human and nowhere near
perfect.
This I'm certain. These are words that may
have reared its head a tad late, but we must
continue our game-
I don't want you-
I don't want you to stop hanging with me.
I don't want you to leave my sight.
I don't want you to catch someone else's
eye.
I don't want you to hit that girl from
behind.
I want you to be mine.
This is not a game and I wish I could say
that one was the lie, but
The question is am I too late this time.

Letdowns and Fears

I search for the faults
Like every dude before and so when
something comes up
I mark it down, there goes a point
Two weeks later and I'm still hurt
Even though I know you thought we
moved on from it
I still feel your unspoken words
I am trying not to let it get to me
To change my mind, heart, and soul
To not put negative impressions
On what the future may hold
But now the smallest things you do is
starting to stain
This spot in my mind that you had begun to
taint
I am hurting which is why I write
Trying to downplay these hard feelings that
I can't seem to shake
I feel unwanted and as if I am waiting
I don't want to be near your home and I
rather just stay away
Since it seems you like it better that way
I was looking forward to your face even
though I am still upset
But my expectations took a dive as you
cancelled again
Said your boys needed help and time
passed, but what about me

I waited for you, but you seem to have
abandoned me
I hate to sound selfish, but what about my
needs
It's great to receive text and for you to ask
me about my day
But I prefer personal contact, I need to see
your face
I am glad you listened to my advice and are
starting to make a change
But lately it seems that you are drifting
further away
My heart is pumping, but my mind is
running wild
Telling me to pull back and watch from the
crowd
Don't put your all in because you are about
to get hurt
So pull back and become distant. Hold your
heart while you still can
It's time to have a back up plan
I hate to think like this because it leads me
to the worst
I become more worried everyday about
getting hurt
I just wish you feel what I feel so I could
stop crying inside
I hate to keep arguing, but my mind has
pulled me aside
I keep silent because I am making my next
move

I just hope you make a play before I decide
to make a game plan without you.

Love Addiction

The way you hold me is addicting
Like crack I pump my veins with your
affection and get high off the warmth
My heart beats fast and the blood rushes
through my veins
At times I think I am insane
I feel your breath on my ear, and I realize
this is reality
Your words are poetry meant only for me
You squeeze me tighter and I lose a little
breath
Sometimes I wanna ask God if this a test
Because I am falling to my death
I need more of you because my tolerance is
growing
You are always on my mind
And even when my focus should be on
other things
All I can think about is my next high
I feel your heartbeat thump against your
chest
I have failed the test
I fill my syringe with your poison while I
count to three
I want to keep this feeling inside me
I relax and let your love encompass my
body
Letting go of my insecurities as I let you see
the other side of me

I hold on to you tighter, so I won't drift
away
But somehow you begin to fade
I may have made a mistake
My high is falling, and I am on my knees
The sound becomes clear and I hear you are
leaving me
Reality hits and I realize your hands are no
longer holding me tight
But rather pushing me away
I quiver at the sound of my name as you
release the syllables from your lips
I ask for one last kiss, one final hit
But you deny, say it's time for you to leave
my side
I cry because my high is now gone
I'm all alone
And all have is an empty syringe
Because the love that was there, is now long
gone.

Realization

I miss you

I try to play hard, but I miss you
It hasn't been long since our bodies been
intertwined
Your fingers looped with mine
Since I laid on your chest and listened to
your heartbeat
And rubbed my hand through your curly
black hair
I miss you
I miss the way you held me when I was
down
Or the way we talked for hours, flowing
through topics
Like water through a faucet
Or the way you would buy me food
Because you knew that always made my day
I miss you
The way we joked and laughed
Always picking on our flaws then claiming
that we were both mean
The way you asked for my advice and I
would tell you the honest truth
The way we shared our dreams and worries
throughout the silent hours of the night
I miss you
The way you kissed me passionately like I
was your only meal

The way you caressed my body and looked
into my soul as a part of your body began to
take up space in mine
The way you became weak under my touch
and my tongue explored your neck
The way you let out a gasp or moan when
my lips wrapped around your dick
I miss you
Even now as I try to forget, I always receive
a text
We talk as if times haven't changed and
things are still the same
It hurts you know, but I continue to be
polite
I miss you, but I know why we did not work
You are impatient and insecure
Always doubting yourself and unsure
You encourage, but only when asked
Never out of the kindness of your heart
You don't brag which is usually ok

But you show off your best friend
Like she is the new slave on the market
You lack the drive that I need in a man
Someone that pushes themselves harder
than I can
I know we did not work
The strength and hard work binwas not
there
I was pulling more weight on my end and
You continued to pretend that you cared

But if that was true, you would have tried
harder boo
You wouldn't have given up if you felt the
person is worth the fight
Not if the relationship is bound tight
I miss you
But I know why we didn't work
So I won't go backwards, but rather
continue to go forward
This was a lesson well learned

Cover Blown

I trusted you, crazy right.
Here I was about to apologize to a snake
that was already slithering.
Dumb right
But you had a good cover, what can I say?
Had me fooled up, wrecked, and mixed up.
Walking on your trail trying to find out
where I fell off at.
I liked you and treated you like a King.
Even gave you the keys to my palace, but
you spat on it.
Forget respect, it's too late for that shit.
Your cover is blown, you're just another
dog out for a bone.
All those late nights you were laying up in
my covers,
Lapping up the remains in my pot, soaking
up the heat in my car
You were really just scratching the sore that
would soon become a scar.
I laugh, but my heart hurts to. Someone you
trust so much turning out to be another
mutt.
Can't say much. I might have trailed you
along at some points, but my wrong doesn't
make yours right.
It just brings yours to the light and damn it's
shining bright. I just couldn't see it behind
that deceiving smile.

I let the fences to my heart open and let the
guard take a break then
That's when you intruded, but I learn from
my mistakes.
There will not be another you again.

<u>Heart of Lies</u>

All she wanted is your attention
To know you cared
But instead you decided
To take your heart and share it
With another girl instead
She waited patiently
Hoping you would change your mind
But little did she know
You were already in the bed with Her this
time

<u>Fake gesture</u>

Your affection is an illusion
It is a painted picture that fades with the day
As the sun goes down so does my pain
Those texts you send are just a copy
A blueprint that has been used again and
again
Your affection is wavering
Lying is a sin

Surprise Ending

You claim to be part of a different breed.
Different than I often perceive
Rather that one lone seed that doesn't
develop with the weeds.
You claim to be one of a kind
One of the treasures that you happen to
find
Lying in the bin at goodwill surrounded by
everyday objects.
You claim that you want to get to know me
From the last time I cried and why I have so
much pride.
These are the claims I used to believe
Before I realized that you are what I
perceived you to be.
Labrador, Husky, pits, and poodles are all
different you see, but
Still are different dog breeds. You might not
be the like the past dudes
, but the apples usually don't fall too far
from the same tree.
I fell into your portals of lies and apologies.
Your I love you's and you're the only one
for me.
Until I realized that was simply a script you
were reading to please .
I saw your ways as you slithered into my
heart,
So that's why I took extra precautions and
set up the bars.

The trick of the game is the one you have
yet to see.
While you tried to get me to fall hard,
You fell harder for me.

The Rise

old you, New Me

My love is insatiable
These words for you is premeditated
I thought you were honest, but now I'm
fixated
On the lies you fed me, aggravated
I gave you the time of day, prorated
And now I wish I could take the hours
back, dissipated
I'm not even mad at you, lesson learned
I set my roster down so I guess you took
that as a point earned
But let's be clear, I'm simply not "another
one"
I can't be transferred or replicated
Your character is definitely tainted
My personality and looks are a rarity
A gift that often provided you clarity
I know you looked back and wished you
seen
The girl you had under your wing
But now
I've gone places you ain't never seen
Catching glares from other guys that
insinuate things
The woman inside is spreading her wings
Moving on and doing things to flourish
This life takes courage
Something you lacked often, but I was
always sure of

This growth is unheard of
I'll make sure to thank you when I'm
illustrious
Because you helped pushed me to shine
even brighter, industrious

<u>Experiences</u>

Right from the beginning I had my heart
broken. It started before you, but I
continued to give love a chance.
Experienced disappointment at a young age,
but I try not to let that discourage me. I
swore that guys I talked to would be
different from my father.
My mother was always there for me though.
Always held me close as tears streamed
down my face and told me, people always
will show who they really are.
Eventually my father realized what he said
and do has long term effects, but it's too
late to apologize or change the past. My
heart has solidified, and my feelings have
become brittle and unrelenting.
Most guys have proven to be just like him
and are more talk than action. There are few
guys that continue to put forth effort after
the initial meeting.
Boys will be boys, but I require a man.
Every good thing takes time and work. If
you don't have the time and work effort,
then keep your compliments to yourself.
Sweet nothings fall on deaf ears.
Right now, the only person I believe is
myself.

Build-A-Man

If I could combine all the men, I dated into
one, I could create a monster
While also making the ideal man
Combining the positive traits would be
idyllic,
But I can't be too picky
One ex was a great listener and a gentleman
But had demons of his own to battle
Another ex was funny and had a good
personality overall
And as a bonus, was pretty good in bed
But was pessimistic, untrustworthy, and
lacked motivation
Another man I talked to briefly was an
overall good catch
He was a gentleman, had his life together, a
loving protector
But in the end turned out to be a cheater
Life is funny right
I could go on and on, but the point is
I'm tired of buying manufactured niggas
Or mass-produced men
Can someone invent build-a-man?
A one in a kind individual that fits my needs
and wants
But still has his flaws
A man that I can trust and that holds the
same morals as me
Not one that tells me he wants to be with
me then goes out on a date

With a "good friend" I have never heard of
before
Not someone that tries to talk to my best
friend after mentioning her ass
Yet claims he was just being friendly
Not someone that tells me to meet them
after I get off a 7 hr work shift
Only to say they are not home, when I get
to their house
Not someone that tells me to be open and
trust them
Or claims they don't have time for games
Yet they have a whole wife at home
Not someone that says, "I don't post you
because I don't want people in our
business"
Or "what hoes"
Yet they have a girlfriend a week after
sexting you
Not someone that waste my time after
requesting it
Not someone that thinks I'm here for
entertainment purposes
Not someone that brings negativity and
stress into my life
Because lately this is all they have to offer
These are real experiences
Different ages, different times in life,
different personalities, totally different
people
But they still all have one commonality
between them all

They are all mass-produced men not worth
more than a piece of a forgotten gum under
a school desk
All this to say is I want a man that is
specially made for me
Not another mass-produced mistake

Don't I Deserve

I dedicate this one to my good women out
there
The ones that don't get recognized or
appreciated
The one's that have their ish together, look
bomb effortlessly, and have a good head on
your shoulders
But still get ignored daily
Because they don't flaunt or boast, but
rather wear their crowns in silence.
I applaud because we are doing the right
thing.
We are smart, we are loving, we are
overlooked
Another page in a forgotten book
Another queen that fails to be seen.
It's sad you see. Dudes beg for women that
have it together.
For women who lead, are independent,
For women who are beautiful and smart –
What they call "wifey material", but yet they
continue to chase the women who are
empty shells
As they pass up the strong woman among
them.
They disrespect the gift God personally
delivered to them to follow the next quick
thing that comes through.

Then you have the nerve to turn around
and ask why can't you find a good woman.
She quenched for your attention and did
what she could.
She made time for you in her busy schedule,
but yet you still acted like Bubu the fool.
Then stand there puzzled when she leaves
you with memories of her embedded into
you.
Of what you could have had, but instead
you used her like an old tool.
Good women this is for you because I
understand the pain you go through.
I consider myself to be a good woman too
and you can only put up with so many
valueless boys
Before you realize you are worth much
more and deserve
A man that values everything you do.
So on those days you feel lonely and
consider lowering your standards,
Look forward to the next day and what will
be better.
Because if that man couldn't make the first
cut then that means
He isn't worth recruiting.

Seriana's poetry comes from the soul so many of her pieces are first drafts so that you get the most authentic part of her. If you ever want to share your love experiences or reach out to the author feel free to email her: **serigpoetry@gmail.com**